ECHO
OF
WARS

ECHO
OF
WARS

PROFESSOR M.R. ALI

Matador
5 Weir Road
Kibworth Beauchamp
Leicester LE8 0LQ, UK
Tel: (+44) 116 279 2299
Fax: (+44) 116 279 2277
Email: books@troubador.co.uk
Web: www.troubador.co.uk/matador

ISBN 978 1848761 865

British Library Cataloguing in Publication Data.
A catalogue record for this book is available from the British Library.

Typeset in 11pt Book Antiqua by Troubador Publishing Ltd, Leicester, UK

Matador is an imprint of Troubador Publishing Ltd

Printed in Great Britain by the MPG Books Group, Bodmin and King's Lynn

To the victims of wars

CONTENTS

INTRODUCTION

As an Iraqi born global citizen, I thought of adding my voice to anti-war movements by declaring that no military war is legal.

I have written the poems in 'ECHO OF WARS' for my country in particular and the world at large, to show how much I hate these destructive and murderous wars.

The reader may recognise that these poems were written over a period of time, extending from the first Gulf War until the present day.

ACKNOWLEDGEMENTS

My first acknowledgement goes to poet Laureate Andrew Motion who broke his silence to join the doubters over Iraq in his famous thirty word poem 'Causa Belli' published in *The Guardian* on 9th January 2003.

I realised I was not alone and I also realised that the anti-war marchers all over the world will be proven right one day.

Six years on and the day has come when the British army have quit my country Iraq!

Now I can present my anthology

'*Echo of Wars*'

dedicated to the victims of all wars.

My second acknowledgement goes to Professor T.J.Williams, a life long mentor, who advised me to send a copy of the anthology to President Bush and Mr Tony Blair, on that I am still thinking...

My third acknowledgement goes to Dr Panu Rajala, a distinguished Finnish writer and the senior lecturer Faruk Abu Chacra of the Helsinki University.

My fourth acknowledgement goes to my family and friends, in particular my Daughter-In-Law, Ilona Ali, who checked the manuscript thoroughly.

And my final acknowledgement, and appreciation, goes to the Britsh public whose patience and fair-play attitude are well known, especially through difficult times.

ABOUT THE POET

Take a glance through the following names…

Gilgamesh Epic, 1001 Nights, Shaherazade, Harun Al-Rashid, President Bush, Sinbad the Sailor, Garden of Eden, Babylon, Hammurabi and Nineveh…

These names must remind you of one country?

IRAQ!

From Iraq the famous Arabic poetry came, and so did the poet M.R.Ali.

He has written numerous poems and lyrics in the following published anthologies –

- *Poems of the Cities*
- *Poems for Art's Sake*

His literary work is used effectively as a base for songs and internet broadcasts and musicals. In addition to his poetry writing, he is also the inventor of the Deltar, a musical instrument, as well as starting an art movement called Deltaism, as post cubism.

GOING TO BAGHDAD

Dad Dad, a dream I had
Of going to Baghdad
Lad Lad, I will be glad
To take you to Baghdad

Dad Dad, drawing close from the sky
I see Baghdad from up high
Lad Lad, this is the sight
Of one thousand and one nights

Dad Dad, is this truly the city
Of the Abbassides' dynasty?
Lad Lad, soon you will find
Baghdad has its mind
Shall we swing along the cradle of dreams
Watching the Tigris and Euphrates streams
Past, flowing with memories
Of Mesopotamia's past glories

Dad Dad, lets take the magic carpet ride
With Sinbad as our guide!
Lad Lad, see the top of Mount Ararat
Where the Prophet Noah sat

Dad Dad, touring Nineveh and its splendour
Discovering the Assyrian culture
Lad Lad, lets move south on our tour
To see Sumer and Ur

Dad Dad, hear the Gilgamesh Epic
The tune of the lyre and the lyric?
Lad Lad, now we pass through the garden of Eden
The home of the heartbroken.

Dad Dad, I can see from afar
The great Gate of Ishtar
Lad Lad, from Eden the legacy goes on
To the hanging gardens of Babylon

Dad Dad, was Hammurabi's tablet a fact
With legal impact?
Lad Lad, it is the most ancient code
That was ever told

Lad Lad, great figures from the past
Gave Baghdad its diversity and contrast
Dad Dad, I feel so grand
Touring such a land
Let's rejoice in Baghdad
With the music of Scheherazade

WAR IS A WHORE

War!
What for?
And who wants more?

War!
That we deplore
But the politicians
And arm's dealers adore!

War!
War is a whore!
The generals
Will fall to the floor!

LIBERATION OF KUWAIT

Come, look and wait

The occupation of Kuwait

Created a graveyard

Of misery and hate

Come, look and wait

The liberation of Kuwait

Created a Petro-

Dollar United State

UNITED NATIONS

Destruction of a Nation
By the United Nations
Without the world's authorisation

Destruction of an ancient civilization
By the so-called civilized nations
Is described as liberation

The permanent council members
Dismembering another member
In the name of justice and order!

Security Council, wake up!
A new world order is being set up
Iraq and Kuwait are caught in a trap

Your charter is supreme
Created as a dream
For a global regime

Your charter gave birth to nations
And many global organisations
And now you need a celebration

Congratulations, Mother of all Nations
Back in the Baghdad bombing
An achievement of your doing

Your Mother was the League of Nations
You were born out of frustration
And Bush has determined your destination

DESTRUCTION OF A NATION

A high tech drama
Created a panorama
Of the Gulf melodrama
With a Nostradamus aroma

The high tech distortion
Beyond any imagination
Will create a desperate situation
For the coming generation

The coming generation
Will suffer
Because of what their ancestors
Had to offer

The calamity of confrontation
Of such power and concentration
Is a gross distortion
Of the people's aspiration

Leaders leading wars
As before
Are not attractive
Any more

Leaders should not
Ignore all
The messages of peace and
The writing on the wall

Leaders should listen
To the voice of reason
Before committing
cowardly acts of aggression

War is repulsive
Its price is expensive
The result is destructive
Victory is elusive

Wars have no winners
Only losers and more losers
Do we never learn
From our fallen warriors?

Fighting each other
For no reason whatsoever
Should not be a lesson
For us to remember

The Gulf crisis is a warning
Soon we will be learning
That as the oil boils
The world is burning

The weapons of technology
Will destroy the world's ecology
The war mongers will not
Be saved by an apology

The new world order
Is economic murder
But the rich will get richer
The poor will get poorer

The spiralling rises
Of commodity prices
Depress the world economy
And trigger financial crisis

The Gulf crisis
Is an excuse
For warring powers
To exchange abuse

They only see
The Gulf of difference
Between them through each other's eyes
As a crisis of confidence

They believe in beginnings
A war is not an answer
For solving any differences
Whatsoever

But always remember
War is neither the answer
Nor a justification
To kill one another

Just remember
The bomb on Hiroshima
Was not an answer
But just another dilemma

And if you remember
War is never an answer
Then peace will
Flourish forever

Give me a reason
For waging war
And I will give you far more reasons
For loving peace

Give me a reason
For hating peace
And I will give you far more reasons
For hating wars

Have you heard
Of the world wars?
And what
They were for?

Have you heard
Of the arms race?
And what it has done
To the human race?

Have you heard
Of the atom bombs?
And what effect they have
On mothers' wombs?

Have you heard
The wounded crying?
And have you
Cared for the dying?

Have you been
In a war before?
And if so why do you
Want more?

When shall we learn?
If we ever learn
Not to make the same mistakes
Again and again

War or no war
The question is for us all
Give wisdom a chance
And let peace be our goal

ON THE WAY TO HEAVEN

I am the pushy Bush,
Who are you?

I am the sadistic Saddam,
Do I know you?

Yes you do!
And I must confess
Did we not work together?
To make that mess

I don't remember!
Do you mean the new world order?

Yes, yes
The new world order
Now in progress

I wonder
If I will be remembered
As a martyr
Forever

Yes, yes
You have done your best
To be remembered
By the rest

I am glad I encouraged you
To bomb Baghdad
Now you and I
Can declare a victory
With your courage and mine
We have written history

Yes, yes
This makes sense
Now I am a war hero
For my people and the press

Yes
You are the father of all heroes
Married to the mother of all battles

Oh!
What a romantic and poetic
Leader you are,
A charming superstar

We went that far
Understanding each other
And poor Mrs Thatcher
Kept on nagging forever

Never mind
She did not understand
What was in my mind
She read the situation
And started the condemnation

Condemnation of what?!

The Kuwait occupation
Out of her frustration

You did not give her
Any indication

What indication?

Of our secret negotiation

What negotiation?

Of James Baker's initiation

You mean Ambassador Gillespie?

Yes
The poor Gillespie
Where is she?

I don't care
About other people's affairs
All I care about
Is my family and presidency

What a funny feeling
I feel the same
I am not ashamed

Ashamed of what?!

I mean, I'll do anything
For my family
And my presidency
I go to war
And I go to peace
As I please
As long as I stay in one piece

You are a gambler

Does it matter?
We are all gamblers
In the Middle East theatre

You are clever

Of course
I deal with petro-dollars

How much is the rate?

For you
Not much

Now I feel happy
My soul is travelling
To eternity
Let us remember
The happy days
When I was bombing
What were you doing?

I was in a bunker
Hearing the sounds
Of explosions
With excitement
And emotion

I wish I had been
With you

In the night
Baghdad was lit
Like candlelight
Just right
Vibrating to the tune
Of carpet bombing
Like a disco rocking

I wish I had been
With you
To dance the night through

It would have been nice
To toast each other's desire
Under friendly fire
That would have been
Marvellous
Dancing all night to
The melody
Of Baghdad and
Her tragedy

Now I feel better
I wish I had
Met you earlier

We did!
Don't you remember?!

Yes I do remember
But why did we quarrel
With each other?

You must remember
We were only players

That is right
You were all the time
In my sight

That is right
I forgot for a while

Don't you remember?
The extra mile
And the invitation
To diffuse the situation

What invitation?

Tariq Aziz?

The one you wanted
To tease!

And James Baker?

The oil dealer!

Now you see how
Sincere I was?

If you were then why
Did you not invite me?

Where?

To the White House

For what?

To kick my arse

Yes, I should have done that
But it is too late now

I could have come with
My white horse
As a special guest
Of course
Then Congress endorses
A division of oil resources

Why did nobody mention that to me?

I was scared of you
When you were nervous
I tried to calm you down
I sent you King Hussain

The clown!
He did not wear his crown!

I sent you messages
During my prayers
We are two main players
In the New World order
What about Premier Shamir?
What about Emir?
What about Arafat?

I hated Arafat as a player
With his beard
He looked so weird
He was on your side
But I am glad
You took him for a ride!

Come on mate!
What about Mubarak
Assad and King Fahad?
And your coalition
Wasn't that a farce?

Now we are together
Wouldn't it be better
To speak about
The next adventure?

You mean
We bluff
The gate keeper?

That is exactly what I mean
I have an idea
Let's disguise our identities
First we must change
Our names

To what?

To Far Eastern names
Such as Bushbabo the Bright!

That is clever
Then my name shall be
Sadbabo the Sunny!

What have we been doing?
Down there on earth

Playing!

In a band, I guess
We entertain people!

We should call the band
'Cruise Baby Cruise'

That is suitable, but
Now we need a song!

Okay, what about
'Down by the Rubicon Side'?

But the gate keeper
Will not know that!

Isn't that better?

No! We must not confuse him
We must call our song
'Down by the Narrow and
The Straight Side'

Look! Look!
I see the gates of Heaven
Our turn is approaching
We will soon be celebrating
In Paradise

'Let me do the talking,
And you do the smiling'

What language do they speak?

English of course, just watch!
'Hi Mr Angel!
My name is Bushbabo the Bright
And may I introduce
My co-player
Mr Sadbabo The Sunny?'

(But they realise their dialogue
Had been overheard!
For the CIA of Heaven had
Listened to their conversation)

I hear voices out there
They say we are sinners

'Yes, you are sinners'
The angel replies
'You must go down to Hell!'

I just came from there

I was looking forward to
This trip of retirement

'We know who you are'
The angel cuts him short

You see, bloody Bushbabo
You always lie to the
American people

You, bloody Sadbabo
Also lied to the
Iraqi people

'Okay, we've decided to send you back
From where you came
Today is a special forgiveness day'
The angel intervenes

Oh no!
Who would want us back?

(Bush intervenes)
We can tell them
We just returned
From Paradise
With self-sacrifice
To start a new enterprise!

Let me apologise
To Mr Angel
And ask if he can cancel…

'Cancel what?!'
A loud voice came
From the gate of Heaven
'Angel Trabeal of repatriation
Will take you back
From where you came'
The voice obdurately went on

Oh boy!
They mean business
Perhaps I should
Have entered alone
As the Leader of the Free World!
And left the
Bastard Sadbabo to
Himself

Hey you Bushbabo, you should
Be happy!
We are not in real Hell
Now we can live
New lives of our choice
What about you?
Why don't you descend on earth
As Abraham Lincoln?
I will go down as Saladin
To lead my people again

(Bush replies)
I really fancy
Being the King of Arabia
Living forever with my Harems
And my dreams
And the petro-dollar to take care
Of all my expenditure…

Perhaps, I will go to America
As the new Martin Luther King
And to the American people
I shall bring happiness, pride
And many other things

It sounds good to me
Let us see and agree

You mean Angel Trabeal
Where will he be?

No! No!
I am wondering
Who will pay the fee?

Don't worry about that
More important is to ask
How should we flee
And make ourselves free?

I got it! I got it!
We can tell Angel Trabeal
That we need to go to the bathroom
And then we will be free

You see,
You American Presidents
Have the answer for everything
You are so clever

Angel Trabeal was listening
He let them go to the bathroom
His mission had ended
Now Bushbabo and Sadbabo
Are on their way to the bathroom
To start new lives

As they emerge
See what they find!
A guard is waiting
To arrest them

No! No!
You cannot
Arrest me

(The guard nicely replies)
'We found a nice home back on earth
For you, Bushbabo
And your friend, Sadbabo'

Look!
Look at your hand!
Look!
Look at your face!
(Saddam to Bush)

What?

You look like a monkey!

You also look
Like a monkey too
Look at your hand

Oh yes it is true
I am
A monkey now too

The guard
Took them to a zoo
To be true monkeys
To the people
They had deceived

UNCLE SAM

Bush Bush flew to Baghdad
With a turkey

On thanksgiving day
He looked like a murky Yankee

Smiling in his military gear
He thinks he is funky

Only two hours stay
And the commander-in-chief was afraid and shaky

He is better than his dad
Who avoided Baghdad

The son will take all of the risks
He is a smart lad

Bringing food and presents
To soldiers who are dispirited

Bush Bush of Baghdad
Soon vanished into the clouds

The American plastic turkey
Flew back safe and glad

He dreamed of descending on Baghdad
Riding on a flying carpet

The Iraqis welcomed him
With contempt and bullets

The strongest man of the world
Behaved like a pathetic and silly twit

Abraham Lincoln you are not
You are Bush the thief of Baghdad…
That is it!

ABUSE OF POWER

When you abuse the power
And become a baby killer
It doesn't matter
If you are the Prime Minister
President or a Leader
You become a criminal

You must know
You are not above the law
And your soldiers
Can refuse your orders
They can say no
Because you are a murderer

Your authority is in tatters
You behave like a dictator
To the Iraqis, you are an invader
And to your citizens, a liar

We all know
You lost the political show
You cannot cling to power
Forever and ever

Please, Sir
Why did you take your country
On the road to disaster?
For this you need to answer!

You are refusing to understand
The world is not safe
In your bloody hands

The world had its share
Of Bush and Blair
Go away you dangerous pair!

PRISON

(In remembrance of notorious prisons such as Abu Ghraib Prison)

Prison is a place of miserable existence
For the people with endurance
Without hope of resistance
And without a voice for remembrance
Is it true?
That to obey is the rule to exist?

Or is it a world of the unwanted
Who wanted to take part
And fell hard and fell apart
Who failed to make it from the start?
Is it true?
That to obey is the rule to exist?

Prison is the place not to be
For whatever the reason may be
Or is it the place to be?
If you have no home and no family
Is it true?
That to obey is the rule to exist?

Like the zoo is a jail
For the beasts which were captured
To protect us from them at first
And to love them sometime later
Is it true?
That to observe is the rule to exist?

Such prisons became famous
For the various inmates' names
All visitors started filing in
To watch the wild games
Is it true?
That to observe is the rule to exist?

Now all the beasts are relieved
No appeal and no defence
Life sentences for them all
All the cells have become homes
Is it true?
That to observe is the rule to exist

Now life starts to be normal
Rehabilitation starts early
And the future seems bright
All the beasts start singing
Is it true?
That to obey is the rule to survive?

For their journey of defection
From the wilds to their homes
They were welcomed
As heroes, but for crimes never done
Is it true?
That to obey is the rule to survive?

Now the days start as normal
Every beast has a schedule
To parade for its living
Telling stories of its past
Is it true?
That to obey is the rule to survive?

Every guard is now a guide
Translating all he knows
About his animals
For the public to enjoy
Is it true?
That to obey is the rule to survive?

Every inmate has a story in a file to remember
Whether a lion or a tiger as a killer
Now they are checked and watched all the time
To ensure a crime doesn't occur
Is it true?
That to forget is the rule to survive?

In celebration of the tree day
Well behaved elephants were reprieved
The rest were reminded of their past
Destroying forests and knocking down trees
Is it true?
That to forget is the rule to survive?

All the beasts have neighbours
But the zebra doesn't like them
All he does is kick and bite
Like a donkey in a fight
Is it true?
That to forget is the rule to survive?

All the monkeys are accused
Of stealing and of funny dealings
It doesn't really matter
As all the guests like monkey business
Is it true?
That to forget is the rule to survive?

What is the fault of the crocodile?
It is questioned all the time
For smiling and never weeping
For the victim who it drowned
Is it true?
That to forget is the rule to survive?

Is it lawful for a parrot
To be caged?
For its mimicry of the ones
Who were outraged?
Is it true?
That to forget is the rule to survive?

When we rule, we need subjects
When we fight, we need soldiers
When we conquer, there are the vanquished
All such actions create prisoners
Is it true?
That to forget is the rule to survive?

Like the wars we fought before
Created heroes, created villains
Wars of all types create prisoners
What can you do with such people?
Is it true?
That to survive is the rule for destruction?

Did you hear of the prisoners of war?
In their thousands
They surrender
And are perhaps exchanged sometime later
Is it true?
That to survive is the rule for destruction?

Such war prisoners have no trial
All are convicted as they arrive
Some are tortured and some are slaughtered
Their only crime was to obey orders
Is it true?
That to survive is the rule for destruction?

Even now, people fight
To achieve feeble aims
Using forces of destruction
Losing all their human values
Is it true?
That to survive is the rule for destruction?

All prisoners need prisons
All prisons are institutions
For all reasons
From detentions to executions
Is it true?
That to forgive is the rule to exist?

Such an institution is tailored
To be rigid, to be tight
To be stiff and to be stern
That is why it is a prison
Is it true?
That to forgive is the rule to exist?

Some prisons used to be castles
Others, lush and pretty islands
Not to speak of the usual places
Labour camps and lifeless buildings
Is it true?
That to forgive is the rule to exist?

Everybody has realised
Such institutions need correction
Need attention
To realise their true function
Is it true?
That to forgive is the rule to exist?

Such a task is not so easy
Such a place has a difficult function
For the correction of human actions
Inherited from previous generations
Is it true?
That to forgive is the rule to exist?

All inmates are customers
To be served without complaints
For a service without tips
And hard labour without thanks
Is it true?
That to forget is the rule to relax?

All arrive with a number
And a file
With a guard and cell allocated
For your comfort
Is it true?
That to forget is the rule to relax?

As a client without choice
Without bills to be paid
All are free of all charges
All you do is wait and think
Is it true?
That to forget is the rule to relax?

Every day passes slowly
Most inmates are friendly
But you feel quite lonely
As your feelings are not with you
Is it true?
That to forget is the rule to relax?

All we need to do is rethink
To find an answer
A hypothetical one is just for fun
Just assume a prison-free world
Is it true?
That to be silent is the rule to be free?

Wars and fights, they go together
Prisons and prisoners for each other
Why don't we have one
Without the other?
Is it true?
That to be silent is the rule to be free?

We can have war without force
We can have fights without losers
And we can have prisoners without a prison
Just imagine earth is heaven
Is it true?
That our earth is a prison for us all?

WIDOW OF THE WAR

Oh Samantha!
Widow of the war
Steve will come back
No more, no more

Oh Samantha!
Steve is a victim
Of the war
Let the voice of reason
Go higher and higher
Than the 'Enemy Fire'
Or the 'Friendly Fire'

Oh sweet Samantha!
Widow of the war
Steve is not coming back
He has completed his mission
Now let us stop the killing
We all are willing

Oh sweet Samantha!
Widow of the war
Steve is calling
War is destruction
And because war is not the answer
People suffer

Oh sweet Samantha!
Widow of the war
Let us silence the gun
The anti-war march has begun
In Steve's memory
Let us make war history

Oh Samantha!
Please lead the call
Let us all stop the war
Let politicians and generals
Fall to the floor

ORPHAN OF BAGHDAD

Orphan of Baghdad
Don't be sad, be proud!
One day you will be in charge
Of your beautiful ancient land

Orphan of Baghdad
Lost Mum and Dad
You are not the only lad!
Lonely Iraqi children
Will not be forgotten…

You started a mission
For the world to listen
Iraq is tragedy written
And we will learn from this hard lesson!

The past is done
The future has begun
Let us silence the gun
In peace we can have fun

Peacemakers on the march
In their millions everywhere
Mr Bush and Mr Blair
Do you really care?

Iraqi orphans, never say never!
Look forward to the future
Soon you will find…
Many youths of your kind

Let your vision
Be a world peace mission
With candles of hope!
Rivers of peace that never cease to flow

A new dawn is born
From the river of Babylon
Around the world to the Amazon
The world's orphans are not alone

Carpet bombing of Baghdad city
Is a sign of barbaric cruelty
World 'Peace Day'
Is the only way
To eliminate shadows of fears
And the misery of wars
Cheers!

BRAVE SOLDIER
(SOLDIER OF PEACE)

Brian is a brave soldier
Who created a political fever
When he told the prime minister
You are becoming a monster

Brian is a brave soldier
With a loud speaker
He told Tony Blair
That he is a liar and a baby killer

Tony Blair did not answer
Because he is shoulder to shoulder
With another murderer
But Brian is a brave soldier

From Parliament Square
Brian played it right and fair
But Mr Blair didn't want him there
The police eviction took him off the air

Artists of the Tate became aware
Brian's manifestation is an artistic affair
His installation became the centre of attention
Of respect and adulation

The story of Brian the soldier
Will be told over and over
Don't follow a blind order
Because you will be judged in the future

Now let us say-
Brian the soldier
Is cleverer
Than his Prime Minister

HOMAGE TO BAGHDAD

Homage to Baghdad
The brave city
Glory to Baghdad
The defiant city

Baghdad is the name
War is the game
Baghdad will be back
Just the same

We know you well
The aggressor will fail
'Hulago' before –
And 'Bush' as well

REMEMBERING IRAQ

Remembering Iraq
Wiped out of the map of memory
Denied its history
Brought to its knees
In the name of democracy
                    Remembering Iraq
                    Deprived of its dignity
                    Atrocity after atrocity
                    Baghdad became a ghost city
                    After Abu Ghraib calamity
Remembering Iraq
What it used to be
From Hammurabi to Al-Mutanabi
A learning place
For all the human race
                    Remembering Iraq
                    From Babylon to the Green Zone
                    Everything has gone
                    It gave the giving
                    And now it is begging

Remembering Iraq
From the cradle of civilization
To the mother of all manifestation
Iraq will return to
its rightful destination

Homage to Iraq
The bravest country
We know you well
Century after century
The aggressor had failed

MISSION ACCOMPLISHED

Missiles intercepted
By the shoes!!!

We heard it on the news!

That is

The end